THE VAGABOND

CURSED TO WANDER

CHANTE ROBINSON

WESTBOW
PRESS®
A DIVISION OF THOMAS NELSON
& ZONDERVAN

WestBow Press books may be ordered through booksellers or by contacting:

WestBow Press
A Division of Thomas Nelson & Zondervan
1663 Liberty Drive
Bloomington, IN 47403
www.westbowpress.com
844-714-3454

Scripture taken from the King James Version of the Bible.

Scripture quotations taken from The Holy Bible, New International Version® NIV® Copyright © 1973 1978 1984 2011 by Biblica, Inc. TM. Used by permission. All rights reserved worldwide.

ISBN: 978-1-6642-3483-3 (sc)
ISBN: 978-1-6642-3484-0 (e)

Library of Congress Control Number: 2021909992

Print information available on the last page.

WestBow Press rev. date: 06/17/2021

CONTENTS

Introduction

Hello, my name is Chante Robinson. I am a wife and a mother of three beautiful children. I was given this assignment to write this book some time ago. I started writing and then I stopped; it was my usual normal routine of starting a thing and then stopping and not finishing. I didn't think much of it because *ehhhhh, it's no big deal!* It was just an idea, right?

Yes, it was God who told me to write. He gave me this task, but for what? I mean, what will this really accomplish? I've always known I had preordained books in my loins, but so far my life has been unproductive—in my opinion, at least. What's the big deal now? Why stop this winning streak I'm on?

Well, one night, while preparing to enter into consecration with the intent of leaving the old year and starting the new year right, I began praying. I began to hear a song in my spirit, and then worship began to pour out of me. I was sobbing and repenting so wholeheartedly and I believe in that moment I touched heaven!

After sobbing, snottin, snifflin—you know, the works—I got up off the floor and I went to YouTube to look up Juanita Bynum's songs and such. I found some teachings that were talking about business, so I listened to all that I could find on the matter. When I was finished, I came across a series of teachings called "The Finisher," and *my God* from that point on things got very interesting!

For the sake of not boring although not boring at all, you I won't go into to details I've given you the title of the teachings feel free to watch for yourselves. I tell you God began to deal with me about some unfinished business I had concerning his business and the things he told me to do. This was not pretty. I was being rebuked and chastised for my insubordination and out right rebellion!!! One of them was to write this book. What could I say to the Lord I was in error? I was not compliant with this work nor have I been with several other works he had given into my hands for some time now.

I was tasked to write this book before the year ended it is now 2020 and I have three days to present to him a finished work. I said God how can this be done? His exact words were you're going to burn the midnight oil and burn the midnight oil is exactly what I did. I fell asleep to writing and typing with the work in my bed next to my pillow, I woke up with that same work in my bed next to my pillow. I was at it again no coffee or breakfast first just working to finish what he told me to start.

I present this book to you as a proud finisher of the work he called me to do in the form of this book. While there is still more for me to do, I have completed this task that I was commissioned with and I am proud of this finished work. I tell you truly that this book is so near and dear to my heart because it was one of the things that God revealed to me was at work in my life and had been for a long time. I tell you that this will bless your life and if you allow God to use this book as a tool it can free you and you then can help free others.

If you find yourself anywhere in this book no matter the chapter, paragraph or page I want you to know that there's nothing too hard for God and all things are possible to them that believe. Don't be overwhelmed by your imperfections because we serve a perfect God!

I wish that you may be as I am free and on the road to recovery in all areas of your life and because there is always room for improvement I seek to stay in a surrendered position allowing the potter to mold me as he sees fit. I pray you enjoy this book and that you are never the same again. May that same yoke breaking anointing that rest over my life preside over yours as well in Jesus's name, amen, and so be it!

The Beginning
of the Curse

Let's start with Genesis chapter 4. The narrative of Cain and Abel is shared with us:

> And Adam knew Eve his wife; and she conceived and bare Cain and said I have gotten a man from the Lord. And he again bare his brother Abel and Abel was a keeper of sheep, but Cain was a tiller of the ground. And in the process of time it came to pass that Cain brought of the fruit of the ground an offering unto the Lord.
>
> And Abel he also brought of the firstlings of his flock and of the fat thereof. And the Lord had respect unto Abel and to his offering.
>
> But unto Cain and to his offering he had no respect. And Cain was very wroth and his countenance fell.
>
> And the Lord said unto Cain, why art thou wroth? And why is thou countenance fallen?
>
> If thou doest well, shalt thou not be accepted? And if thou doest not well sin lieth at the door. And unto thee shall be the desire and thou shalt rule over him.
>
> And Cain talked with Abel his brother; and it came to pass when they were in the field that Cain rose up against Abel his brother and slew him.
>
> And the Lord said unto Cain, where is Abel thy brother? And he said I know not am I my brother's keeper.
>
> And he said what hast thou done? The voice of thy brother's blood crieth out to me from the ground.

And now art thou cursed from the earth which hath opened thou mouth to receive thy brother's blood from thy hand.

When thou tillest the ground it shall not henceforth yield unto thee her strength; a fugitive and a vagabond shalt thou be in the earth. (Genesis 4:1–12)

So right away we see that both the brothers had a responsibility to present God with the choice fruits of their harvests. Both brothers brought their offerings to the Lord, and they presented those offerings to him. God observed their offerings and received one and rejected the other. God accepted Abel's offering and rejected Cain's offering. Why? Why was Cain's offering rejected?

The Word says that Abel brought of the firstlings of his flock and the fat thereof. Cain brought his offering, but God had no respect for his offering. The Word doesn't even say what God thought about Cain's offering. Could he have rejected Cain's offering because of the posture of Cain's heart, or did he choose to reject Cain's offering due to its physical presentation? We don't know because the Word of God does not disclose to us what God's thought process was. What was it about Abel's offering that got God's attention and in the same breath put a bad taste in God's mouth concerning Cain's offering?

Cain did not take this news well, and it caused him to make a decision out on anger, fear, and maybe even envy. It was a hasty decision. A decision that cost him his life. No, Cain didn't die a physical death, but he died a spiritual death. Abel was killed for something that was out of his control. Cain killed his brother over something that could have been fixed. God told him if he did well, he would be received, so why didn't Cain choose to ask God what he needed to change or fix? No matter the reason, Cain made his choice, and it was one that he no doubt regretted!

Cain's Condition

Cain being cursed from the earth made it impossible for him to be established or settle down anywhere on the earth. The earth would not yield her strength unto Cain, resulting in poverty. The earth obeyed what God commanded it to do. God deals with the sin of disobedience when we don't repent with a curse, and that curse brings death. I want to make this point very clear: God is not going around passing out curses like candy to all who make mistakes or miss the mark the first time around or even the second time. It is when we habitually sin, when we disobey and do not repent, that we bring the curse of death on our own heads.

> Romans 6:23 says for the wages of sin is death; but the gift of God is eternal life through Jesus Christ our Lord.

See how we are subject to the curse of death if we choose to allow sin to rule and govern our lives? The wages are the price we pay for our sins. Death is the price for indulging in sin. Death is not something that always happens in physical form as a result of sin but we can die spiritually if we are not careful to obey God in all things. If we take a close look at our lives, I'm sure we can find some areas that are lifeless (dead). The vagabond feels this deeply. If this spirit is at work in your life, you may be wondering why things never work. Why aren't you prospering? My friends, this may be the culprit.

While we are familiar with the narrative of Cain and Abel, there is another story that we are very familiar with as well, and it is that of Moses and the children of Israel and how they wandered in the wilderness for forty years on a journey that in reality took less than a month to accomplish.

The book of Numbers talks about the children of Israel and how they were brought out of Egypt with a mighty hand. God used Moses to return to the land of Egypt and bring his chosen people out of bondage—a bondage that they had been in for four hundred years.

God finally revealed to the people that he heard their crying, their moaning and their groaning and he was coming to their rescue. When Moses arrived with the good news the people were unsure. Some were upset and some were happy to hear that freedom was just a moments time away. We all know the story of how GOD used signs and wonders to deliver the people out of the hands of pharaoh. Let's fast forward to speed things up a bit. They have been freed from bondage on their way to the land that GOD promised them. A land flowing with milk, honey, green grass you name it!

GOD does not give them the details of the journey but commands that they walk by faith and trust him. He feeds them manna from heaven, he gives them the angels bread. Talk about impressive! I mean he has rolled out the red carpet for his chosen bride, no expense spared. When they got bored with the Mana God provided they started complaining and asking GOD for meat. He rains down Quail from the sky every day for them and that wasn't enough. GOD became very wroth with his people because of their unappreciative and ungrateful nature and to top that when Moses leaves to commune with

GOD on the mountain they become bored once again and start building idols to entertain themselves all while provoking GOD to anger.

GOD deals with this because of Moses's constant state of repentance for the people BUT there comes a time when GOD says enough is enough. GOD let's Moses know the plans he has for his people. I am going to kill them, all of them! No one will live and enter into this promised land except for Joshua and Caleb.

> *Numbers 14:35-38*
> *35. I the Lord have said, I will surely do it unto all this evil congregation, that are gathered together against me; in this wilderness they shall be consumed, and they shall die.*
>
> *36. And the men which Moses sent to search the land, who returned and made all the congregation to murmur against him, by bringing up slander upon the land,*
>
> *37. Even those men that did bring up the evil report upon the land, died by the plague before the Lord.*
>
> *38. But Joshua the son of Nun and Caleb the son of Jephunneh, which were of the men that went to search the land, lived still.*

So, we see in this narrative GOD was wroth or angry with the children of Israhel because of their complaining, murmuring, ungratefulness and unbelief. Both Cain and the children of

Israhel suffered the same fate but under different circumstances. We can curse ourselves not only by the shedding of innocent blood without cause, but we can curse ourselves by inhabiting the spirit of unbelief, complaining, ungratefulness, rebellion and murmuring. There are many different reasons why a curse can come upon our lives but today we are just focusing on the curse of the vagabond the wanderer.

I want to share another detail with you that is very important. This curse as well as any others can come upon your life because of direct sin before GOD on your part and it can also be a result of generational curses operating in your life through your bloodline. In the chapters to come you will learn more about what this spirit is and how to overcome it by the blood of JESUS CHRIST! I wanted to set the foundation to give you an understanding of how this curse was implemented in the lives of GODS people in the word of GOD. This is not some incurable disease or a spirit that can't be dispelled and cast out. Deliverance from this spirit like all other spirits is a choice. While there are other steps you have to take this is by far the first and most important of them all. Once you identify this spirit is working in all or some of your life, choose to admit it and then you must desire to be free. We'll talk about the other steps as we continue the journey.

What is a Vagabond?

A vagabond is a wanderer; it is a person with no fixed dwelling place; no fixed direction; a vagrant; a tramp; a person who wanders from place to place, city to city, husband to husband, wife to wife, job to job, church to church etc. This type of person generally doesn't belong to any organization and if they do they are not rooted and grounded within the organization. They can take flight at the drop of a dime just up and move on a whim with no real time put in prayer concerning their decisions. To add to that if they've prayed they were not able to be still and wait on GOD to receive a definite answer from him about what to do concerning their situation, so they move without clear instructions.

They may even consider themselves to be a free spirit not subject to anyone or anything but themselves by their own definition. They lack insight into their lives because they cannot be still enough for GOD to give them insight. They are drifters; stragglers; degenerates and their ways are unestablished. Often they find that they are not able to fit in anywhere always in search of a home but finding none. In worse case cinereous they can lead unsettled, irresponsible and disreputable lives. However, there are some functioning vagabonds just as there are functioning addicts.

The Vagabond

Let's be clear the vagabond is not a person it is a spirit that comes upon a person in the form of a curse and causes them to wander about for most if not all of their lives, if not identified and cast out.

A person with a vagabond spirit doesn't usually detect it right away they are normally unaware of what has befallen them so they have no real way to counter act the attacks they suffer under this curse because they are blind to it's presence in their lives.

A person who deals with this spirit is not established. They are not focused or fixed on one purpose because they cannot be not because they choose not to be. As a result, they are never able to settle in the right place, relationship, calling, job etc. A vagabond is a double minded person.

> **James 1:8- a double minded man is unstable in all his ways.**

Unfortunately, a person who encounters this spirit is not able to bear fruit like GOD desires because they have no roots, this is all due to their wandering. So, by now you may be thinking this book has to be for unbelievers because believers can't have a curse on their lives, and to that I ask why not?

Why can't a believer have a curse upon them? GOD himself lets us know through his word that we have a choice.

> *Deuteronomy 11:26-28 says Behold I set before you this day a blessing and a curse,*

27. A blessing if you obey the commandments of the Lord your GOD, which I commanded you this day,

28. And a curse if ye will not obey the commandments of the Lord your GOD; but turn aside out of the way which I command you this day, to go after other gods which you have not known.

You see every day we are given this gift of life we have a choice and the outcome of your life depends on the choices that you choose to make. Now I do want to add this, you can deal with this spirit not because of what you have done but because of your ancestors or your parents, even your grandparents. If this spirit has not been denounced and cast out this spirit still has the legal authority to operate in your life right now today because of generational curses brought on by your forefathers.

Really and truly this spirit is that of the old man. It is carnal, fleshly, sensual, innate and unrenewed. It is not the born-again part of you it is the part of you that is still being easily beset by sin. It's the man that we never buried the man that we refuse to shed. This man is not able to obey GOD or trust him fully because it is always being opposed and always being hindered. The desire to resist the enemy is always present but the problem is you don't know it's the enemy that's opposing you. YOU don't know that a curse is at work in your life so it's like your beating the wind. Trying to understand things that go against your natural comprehension.

1 Corinthians 9:26- Paul says I therefore so run, not as uncertainly, so fight I not as one that beateth the air.

27. But I keep my body and bring it into subjection; lest that by any means, when I have preached to others I myself shall be a castaway.

The NIV says "Therefore I donot run like someone running aimlessly. I donot fight like a boxer beating the air.

27. He says "NO I strike a blow to my body and make it my slave so that after I have preached I myself not be disqualified for the prize.

It is important in any fight to know your opponent and who or what you are up against. Not so fear can grip you but so you can prepare. This will allow you to know the measures you need to take as well as what equipment you need to bring or use to get the job done!!!!!

Poverty is another friend of the vagabond as well as unaccountability, hopelessness, failure, frustration and so much more! We will get into the meat and bones of the host of other spirits that travel with the vagabond spirit because this spirit does not come alone or in peace. Journey with me a little while longer. I promise you it is well worth your time to understand what has been defeating you so you no longer are beating at the wind but so that you rise to the occasion and make this devil your slave underneath your feet where he is meant to be.

Psalms 23

1. *The Lord is my sheperd ; I shall not want*
2. *He maketh me to lie down in green pastures; he leadeth me beside the still waters.*
3. *He restoreth my soul; he leadeth me in the paths of righteousness for his name's sake.*
4. *Yea thou I walk through the valley of the shadow of death, I will fear no evil; for thou art with me; thy rod and thy staff they comfort me.*
5. *Thou preparest a table before me in the presence of mine enemies; thou anointest my head with oil; my cup runneth over.*
6. *Surely goodness and mercy shall follow me all the days of my life; and I will dwell in the house of the lord forever.*

Through Psalms 23 I've just prepared you for the journey of walking through the shadow of the valley of death so you can kill what's been trying to kill you! You will hit and not miss!

Walk with me now child!

Many Ideas

Just when you thought you found the perfect spot to settle in, the perfect business to start, the right idea to pitch you begin running. Now your off to the races and then something happens, you get a new idea, a better pitch and you just feel like you don't have a place here anymore. What happened??? All of a sudden, you've shifted gears without notice, just suddenly and then your off in another direction. This goes on and on until your feeling confused!

You say to yourself what's going on. I was on my way what happened? What's wrong? Why didn't I accomplish this or that? Why didn't I finish that? Eventually this becomes a way of life and that frustrates you because you realize that you are getting older, you planned on having something to leave behind for your children and you have nothing. Nothing to show for your many travels and good ideas. You have started work but not a finished work. The vagabond is always on the hunt for something new. Deeply longing to obtain a sense of accomplishment, to be settled and enjoy the fruits of their labor but it cannot. The doorway of peace has been shut off and so it wonders in search of an end like being in a desert in search of water after a long day's journey and finding none.

I say it because it is not you it is the spirit that worketh in you. It's the entity that is governing your life or a certain area of your life. It causes its host to not be sound in mind. You may be able to dream but that's all you'll do because it's job is to not allow your dreams to come into reality. So you are constantly bombarded with thoughts, ideas, concepts and ideologies that tickle your ears. You most likely will start the project but not finish because you have no follow through.

There is nothing wrong with being a dreamer. Joseph was a dreamer. However, GOD wants us to bring our work to a completion and in order to do that it takes time and dedication. Which often means that you must be still for a while. GOD wants us to stay the course he has always been the type to lead by example he practices what he preaches. In the beginning when he spoke and began to create all that we see he didn't stop in the middle of creating because he got another idea that was better than what he was working on. He didn't just say you know what this is to hard and it's not turning out the way I planned so I'm going to end this project. No, he stuck it out and saw it all the way through to a finished work!!!

GOD is not whimsical he doesn't frolic in a sea of ideas halted between two opinions and hindered by procrastination and double mindedness. He knows the plans he has for us and he sees it through to bring it to an expected end. All he conceives comes to term and he aborts nothing. Have you noticed that you were gifted to design homes but your selling cars? Or you were gifted to be an engineer but you're stuck in an office. Now sometimes it is what it is and ya gotta do what ya gotta do, I know that but that's not what this is. The vagabond spirit purposely keeps you out of your destined place through wandering. We will miss the mark in this life but if you are a born-again spirit filled believer in JESUS CHRIST and you are actively walking in obedience to him that should not be something that is habitual for you. Wandering is not a characteristic of our Lord!

> *JESUS said in Luke 9:58 "Foxes have dens and birds have nests but the son of man hath no place to lay his head"*

JESUS went from place to place and he still was not a wanderer. He had purpose and he had a plan. The places he went were a part of his purpose and he wasn't testing these places out to see if they would fit in his purpose, he knew they were a part of his purpose from the beginning. When JESUS went to Capernaum, Galilee, Cana, Bethsaida, Judea, Samaria or Perea, he knew what he was going there to do. Whether it be to preach, heal, or do signs and wonders, he knew. Why? Because his purpose was so wrapped up inside of his being that it charted the course for him. There was nothing in him that had to **wonder or wander**.

Even when JESUS went to the Garden of Gethsemane to pray in his final hours before his death, he didn't go there praying to the father saying, father are you sure this is what I'm supposed to be doing? I know you sent me, but these people aren't excepting me will my death really do any good for these people? They seem like they have their minds made up!

No! he said "Abba father, for you all things are possible; remove this cup from me, yet not what I want (**not my will**) but what you want (**but your will be done**). That's the difference. You see, it's not that the wanderer doesn't have or even know their purpose but it's the fact that they are not able to fully walk in it. They may head in the way of purpose but then become easily detoured by other things that take them out of their purpose. This happens time after time again for the person who is dealing with this spirit. This is where the weariness and frustration set in because they think they are well on their way and that they've finally got it and then suddenly there're derailed by their own choices and they don't even realize it. Even if this is happening to you because of a generational curse the effects of this curse are still hindering you presently. It's time to destroy this curse!

> *Jeremiah 29:11 for I know the plans I have for you declares the Lord, plans to prosper you and not to harm you, plans to give you hope and a future.*

When GOD speaks that word does not return to him without a finished work, a result or a completed product.

> *Numbers 23:19 says GOD is not a man that he should lie; neither the son of man that he should repent; hath he said it and shall he not do it? Or hath he spoken and shall he not make it good.*

GOD loves each one of us even those given over to a wandering spirit and those who are dealing with it through a generational curse. He wants us all to be free.

> *2 Peter 3:9 The Lord is not slack concerning his promise as some men count slackness, but is long*

suffering toward us, not willing that any should perish but that all should come to repentance.

If you haven't already realized it is not GOD keeping you from being blessed. You are not banned from your destiny or destined for damnation having received him as your Lord and savior. It is this spirit, this curse working in your life as a hindering spirit and a stumbling block. GOD cannot give you the land he promised you because you would just give it away because you have no roots. If you have found yourself on the pages of this book GOD is speaking to you, letting you know what has been attacking you and that it's not too late to change your life. GOD want you to be grounded in him and we'll discover why through scripture shortly.

So, what does the bible say about the feet of a wanderer?

> **Jude 1:11-13 says Woe to them! They have taken the way of Cain** they have rushed for profit into Balaam's error they have been destroyed in Korah's rebellion.
>
> 12. These people are blemishes at your love feast; eating with you without slightest qualm; sheperds who feed only themselves. They are clouds without rain; **blown along by the wind; autumn tress without fruit, uprooted twice dead.**
>
> 13. **They are wild waves of the sea;** foaming up their shame; **wandering stars;** for whom the blackest darkness has been reserved forever.

The vagabond spirit travels with the spirit of bareness.

Jeremiah 17:7,8

Blessed is the one who trust in the Lord, whose confidence is in him.

8. They will be like a tree planted by the water that sends out its roots by the stream. It does not fear when heat comes; its leaves are always green. It has no worries in a year of drought and never fails to bear fruit.

Psalms 1:1-3

Blessed is the one who does not walk in step with the wicked; or stand in the way that sinners take; or sit in the company of mockers.

2. But whoso delight in the law of the Lord; and who meditates on his law both day and night.

3. That person is like a tree planted by streams of water, which yields it's fruit in season and whose leaf does not wither; whatsoever they do prospers.

Contrary to
Christ

I hope that by now you have a good understanding of the effects of this curse on your life or maybe you have seen some of these characteristics and traits working in someone else's life that you know. Our Lord is all about planting and having roots so that he can produce fruit and harvest it. Everything that he has done since the very beginning was done in a cycle. What do I mean you ask? Well when he created the earth he planted and created things in a way that they would cause the things around it to bring forth on a consistent basis.

Example: in Genesis chapter 1 when GOD made the vegetation and trees, he said "Let the land produce vegetation: seed-bearing plants and trees on the land that bear fruit with seed in it, according to their various kinds". Now the plants and trees that he made both had seed inside of itself so that it would produce or reproduce or replicate itself. Now this happens over the course of time. It takes time to reproduce a thing, so if we are constantly uprooted how can we produce or reproduce anything? God made this earth to be self-sufficient of needing anything else but him. Why? Because of what he placed inside of us.

Take human beings for another example, we reproduce life here on earth. However, we just don't pop out babies everyday as we see fit. No one human being says I want three children right now and I'm just going to command my body to produce them right now and it will be so, and it is so! No! We must go through a process. We have to 1st conceive and then wait for the seed that has been conceived in us to grow and come to full term we must wait. While waiting we nurture and nourish our bodies so that we produce the best offspring that we can.

Our GOD is all about planting and he is a patient man. He could have made all things produce instantaneously but he chose and chooses the timing of all things. He loves to have roots! The character of the vagabond is contrary to GODS character. It shows in every area of their life life or in whatever area of their life life this spirit governs. It is halfhearted in ministry, your worship and your prayer life will reflect this. There will always be something that affects you or offends you and easily I might add, almost everywhere you go! You murmur and complain all the time about most things because your easily offended and all these offenses you encounter lead you to moving your feet out of place or uprooting yourself. It's a vicious cycle and a trick of the enemy!

We must be so careful to be mindful of what we choose to meditate on. Offenses and things that have happened to you via past or present experiences must be carefully and quickly laid at the feet of the father so that he can give us instruction concerning them. Remember whatever we meditate on in our heart becomes the confession of our mouth and whatever we confess with our mouth we give power to bring life or death in our lives. Think of it like this, just like we need a pin to sign a contract to make it binding here on earth we all use our tongues as a spiritual pin and when we speak whatever we speak is binding in the realm of the spirit just like signing a contract is binding here on earth when we use a pin to sign it. Unless we reverse what has been spoken with our tongue as well as reverse what we have signed with a pin we are held responsible for abiding by that contract.

Proverbs 4:23
Keep your heart with all diligence for out of it are the
issues of life.

This scripture speaks to what we all have done and still do some more often than others. It speaks to the murmuring and complaining. We cannot allow this spirit to enter us and spread like a cancer because it is so easy to operate in. This spirit cost the children of Israel everything! Only Caleb and Joshua made it into the promised land! Huh! Why because they were ungrateful and they complained all the time. Nothing was ever good enough for them! They were a hard crowd to impress! They ate manna from heaven, he rained down Quail every day and we not gone even talk about the miraculous signs and wonders of the red sea! I mean what more could he do, well believe it or not we are still behaving like the children of Israhel today! We gotta keep our tongues in check people!

Proverbs 18:21 says Death and Life are in the power of the tongue; and they that love it shall eat the fruit thereof.

The children of Israhel ate the fruit of their tongues and if we be truthful with ourselves, we are eating the fruit of our tongue in some area(s) of our lives as well! Please keep this in mind that this spirit is the catalyst to moving your feet out of place which is why you wander. Now there's other reasons that allow this spirit to operate in our lives, but I believe GOD wants me to highlight this one because it is so prevalent in the earth. With all we have we still want more nothing is ever good enough. We can know that someone next door is doing so much worse than us but we still choose to hold back our praise from GOD and instead give him the fruit of our murmurings and complaining. I know I've been guilty! This is not about condemnation this is about deliverance! It's about repenting and turning away from the things that have kept us wandering for so many years. GOD wants us to be free so much so that he was willing to trade his only son's life for ours!

Let's dig a little deeper........I want to talk about some of the other things that you can expect to be traveling with this vagabond, wandering spirit. We named a few earlier but I want to give you a few more. I think that you will understand further the nature of this beast and why it is so imperative that we rid ourselves of any further dealings or associations with these spirits.

The Curse

Curse- a prayer or invocation for harm or injury to come upon one; a profane or obscene oath or word

Accursed- under a curse; damnable

So, the first place we see the word curse used is in Genesis 3:14 so the lord GOD said to the serpent:

"Because you have done this, you are cursed more than all cattle, and more than every beast of the field; on your belly you shall go and you shall eat the dust all the days of your life."

A curse was used as a pronouncement of judgment on those who break the covenant between them and GOD. In the book of Deuteronomy the bible speaks about curses as a result of disobedience. Wherever you see the word blessing there is also a curse that will follow if you choose not to walk in the blessings of GOD. Now Christ has redeemed us from the curse if we have received him as our Lord and savior but that doesn't mean that we are clear from the curse. Why, because of something called a generational curse.

Curses open the door for many other spirits to enter and bring chaos in our lives in different ways. To give you a more in depth look at some of the things you may see at work in your life here is a short list of some of the spirits that keep company with the vagabond spirit:

Unaccountability- free from accountability or responsibility; lacking the capacity to be given a task that you must complete and give an account, report or answer for.

Instability- lack of stability; the state of being unstable; unpredictable erratic behavior; moody; unreliability; insecure;

shaky. A shaky or unstable foundation is not a foundation that can be built upon with much trust that it will stand. A person that does not have a strong foundation will shift and be tossed to and fro by the storms of life. Because of this you can't build on, or fully trust in a person who possess this characteristic.

Unestablished-This word goes hand in hand with un stability because if you can't be still and take roots you can't become established in anything. To be **established** is to have taken root; it's to be set up or organized; to have a system; to be in a permanent or fixed position indefinitely or for a lengthy period of time.

Unfaithful-not engaging; disloyal; insincere; fickle; deceitful; two-faced; double-dealing; treacherous; false-hearted; unreliable. Need I type anymore!

Unsettled- lacking stability (once again this goes hand in hand with instability and not being established).

Unfinished- not finished or concluded; incomplete; partial or partially done; undeveloped; aborted; half-done; defective; lacking; wanting; patchy; deferred; immature; deficient; put off. Do you see any areas in your life that habitually replicate this word???? Or that stay in constant covenant agreement with this spirit???

Failure-lack of success; miscarriage; abort; frustration; botch; blunder; collapse; catastrophe; letdown.

Frustration- the feeling of being upset or annoyed especially because of the inability to change or achieve something; exasperation; annoyance; anger; vexation; irritation; bitterness; resentment; disappointment; discouragement; depression;

aggravation; discontent; dissatisfaction; the prevention of progress, success or the fulfilling of something.

Run-away- a person who has run away their family, institution or responsibility; fugitive; escapee; deserter; refugee.

Cast-away- thrown away; rejected; cast adrift or ashore; shipwrecked; thrown out or left behind without friends or resources. When we look at this a little closer it is not that GOD has thrown you away. Remember our sins separate us from him. This spirit comes to make you feel you're alone in the midst of your wanderings and even GOD doesn't want you. YOU are NEVER ALONE! It wants you to feel rejected and in some cases we may have been rejected by **GOD BUT NOT BECAUSE HE WANTS TO REJECTS US BUT BECAUSE OF THE SEPERATION THAT MUST OCCUR BETWEEN US AND HIM IF WE CHOOSE TO BE IN COVENANT WITH AND EMBRACE SIN.**

> *Isaiah 59:2 But your iniquities have separated between you and your GOD, and your sins have hid his face from you that he will not hear you.*

Sin creates a barrier between us and GOD he does not waver when it comes to sin. We cannot serve two masters we must choose the one we will serve. We must **LOVE** the one and **HATE** the other there is no other way! Why does such a loving **GOD say that we will either hate the one and love the other or he will hold onto the one and despise (hate) the other?**

If nobody else knows GOD knows that it's a hard thing to

be fully devoted to opposite causes. It's a very difficult thing to hate somebody and love them at the same time whole heartedly. It feels like your being torn apart. Peace comes when you make up your mind about a thing and stick with your decision no matter what it is. The most humbling reason that this loving GOD we serve knows why we have to make a choice and why we can't serve two masters is that guess what? SATAN HATES YOU! He has already made up his mind about you and that won't be changing anytime soon. There is nothing in satan that is shaky or unstable, he isn't wavering in his emotional being for you! Satan doesn't have another word he can use to describe how he feels about you that will sum up the whole of his expression towards you other than HE HATES YOU! HATE, HATE HATE!!!! I digress now I believe you've got it!

> *Matthew 6:24- No man can serve two masters for either he will hate the one and love the other; or else he will hold to the one and despise the other. Ye cannot serve two masters.*

> *Joshua 24:15- and is it seem evil to you to serve the Lord, choose ye this day whom you will serve.*

Rebellious- showing a desire to resist authority; control or convention; defiant; insubordinate; unruly; unmanageable; turbulent; ungovernable; resistant; disobedient.

Selfish-lacking consideration for others; concerned chiefly with concern for one's own profit; lacking care or concern for others; self-regarding; self-obsessed; self-serving;

inward-looking; thoughtless; insensitive; greedy; unmindful; inconsiderate.

Fear-an unpleasant emotion caused by the belief that someone or something is dangerous likely to cause pain or a threat; fright; terror; alarm; panic; agitation; dread; unease; anxiety; distress; worry; timidity; disquiet; doubt; nerves; discomposure; apprehension; foreboding.

When we deal with this word called fear, I'd like to take a different approach. You see all these things that I have here as a definition of fear are really just the symptoms of fear. This is what fear produces in the mind of the one who chooses to meditate on its whispers. Don't be fooled fear has no real authority just like the rest of these spirits except what has been given to it by you and me.

Death-the action of fact of dying or being killed; the end of a life of a person or organism; demise; passing; end; the expiration of a thing; the permanent ending of vital process.

Pain-physical, spiritual or mental discomfort or suffering caused by illness, injury or affliction; soreness; ache; hurt; torment; torture.

Miscarriage-the spontaneous loss of a woman pregnancy; the expulsion of a fetus; from the womb before it is able to survive independently; an unsuccessful outcome of something planned; stillbirth.

Sickness- the state of being still; disease; infirmity;

Lack-the state of being without or not having enough os something; absence; want; need; in-suffiency; scarcity; shortage; deficiency; deficit; inadequacy; famine; drought; poverty.

Procrastination- the action of delaying or postponing something; stalling; hesitation; delating tactics.

Despair-the complete loss or absence of hope; hopelessness; desperation; distress; anguish; pain; dejection; gloom; misery; melancholy; discouragement.

Poverty- the state of being extremely poor; destitution; indigence; the state of being inferior or insufficient in quality or amount; impoverished; hardship.

Business Failure-refers to a company ceasing operation following the inability to make a profit or to bring in enough revenue to cover its expenses. You can be a doing well in start, but something happens to derail your business.

Confusion-lack of understanding; uncertainty; indecision; doubt; the state of being bewildered or unclear in one's mind about something; disorientation; wonder.

Double-Mindedness-double-mindedness is to be inconsistent; to be and act one way today and act one way tomorrow; unstable and unsettled mentally. Lacking solid convictions; lack of understanding.

(this goes so much deeper than just what I have shared with you, double mindedness is spirit that needs to be studied on its own to get the full understanding of the detriment of operating in this spirit).

Murmuring-a subdued or private expression of discontent or dissatisfaction or annoyance about something; complaining.

Grief-deep sorrow; sadness; suffering; affliction; heartache; heartbreak; agony; woe; dejection; bereavement; lament; despair; sorrow of heart.

Suicide-the act of attempting to take one's own life.

Besetting Sins-a main or constant problem or fault; constantly present or attacking; obsessive.

Financial Extortion-the practice of obtaining something especially money through force or threats; the wrongful use of actual violence or intimidation to gain money or property from an individual entity.

Now this term seems so formal in its definition however we can see this spirit at work in the life of the vagabond through not being able to keep money. Either they lack the ability to walk in wisdom in this area and so are making imprudent decisions regarding their finances or they have a mind to act prudently but something keeps happening to literally suck everything they try to save out of their pockets. Remember the palmer and the canker worm this would be their handy work!

Guilt-the feelings of regret; shame; dishonor; disgrace and condemnation.

Hinder-create difficulties for someone or something resulting in delay or obstruction; obstruct; inhibit; thwart; setback; delay; arrest; hold-up; hold-back; restrict; block; curtail; shackle; cripple; constrain; restrain.

Resentment-bitter indignation at having been treated unfairly; displeasure; hard feelings; acrimony; hostility; hate; hatred; enmity.

Unforgiveness-when you are unwilling or unable to forgive someone for hurting, betraying, breaking your trust or causing you intense emotional pain.

Oppression-prolonged cruel or unjust treatment or control;

the state of being subject to persecution; abuse; mental pressure or distress; tyranny; suppression; enslavement; exploitation; injustice; suffering; subjection; subjugation; ill-treatment.

Depression-constant state of sadness, worthlessness, or hopelessness.

Harassment-aggressive pressure or intimidation; pestering.

Scattered-occurring or found at intervals or various locations rather than all together; distracted or disorganized; spread out randomly; tossed about here and there.

These are but a few of the spirits that tag along with the wandering vagabond spirit. You will notice that within these definitions are other words that you may also identify with. I encourage you to be truthful with yourself and examine yourself. Ask yourself .... is this me? Have I been a renegade betraying the principles of GOD and abandoning my post in the spirit, if you do find yourself anywhere on the pages of this book than you've got the first piece of the puzzle? Now you know what you are dealing with!

There is Hope in Jesus Christ the Hope of Glory!

The blessing of the Lord causes us to be rich and wealthy in him, it brings fullness of joy peace and contentment. We are promised to receive the inheritance of GOD if we walk in his ways and follow his precepts. Obedience to GOD brings life the curse brings death, both are rewarders of those who choose their pathway.

In JESUS CHRIST we are no longer under the law of the flesh. We are no longer children of perdition. We are adjured by our Lord to live holy and righteous lives before him, making wise choices proving that which is good, acceptable and pleasing in his sight according to his word.

We need not fear but only walk in humility with a repentful heart. If what you have read resonantes with your spirit we have some work to do. Thankyou Lord you have allowed us to know what has been attacking us! Now its time to repent, denounce, renounce and break all covenants associations and contracts that we have made with these spirits knowingly and unknowingly. That means that all covenants established with Satan through mutual consent or through bloodline attachments must be destroyed! Sever all soul ties to anything that directly or indirectly correlate with any of these damned spirits.

Freedom is not only ours because of JESUS CHRIST but freedom is ours for the asking! Let's investigate what it means to denounce and to renounce.

Denounce means to publicly declare to be wrong or evil. Dispose which simply means to get rid of or throw away.

Renounce means to declare one's abandonment of a claim or right or possession; reject; refuse; resign a tight or position; surrender.

Sever-put an end to a connection or relationship; break off; discontinue; conclude; dissolve; end; stop; suspend; **terminate**.

Cast-Out-get rid of because you do not like or want something or someone in your life; **throw away forcefully**.

Repent- to feel or express sincere remorse or deep regret about one's wrongdoing or sin; see the error in one's way; to turn away from.

Renew-re-establish or reaffirm a relationship; reinstate; revive; resurrect; stimulate; awaken; wake-up; resume after interruption.

Transform-make a thorough or dramatic change in the appearance or character of a person place or thing; rebuild; rework; re-order; metamorphose; convert; transfigure; change.

So here we have it, the recipe for deliverance. **First, identify** what's fighting against you and allow GOD to reveal to you if this is something that you have embraced indirectly as a result of a generational curse or directly as a result of your own disobedience to him.

Second, repent of your sins. Deeply express to GOD the sorrow that has filled your heart as a result of this sin and how you have caused him pain and then turn away! Don't look back!

Third, denounce the sin. Publicly open your mouth and address where you have errored or what has been invading your blood line. This doesn't mean that you have to tell the world, but you need to speak with this matter before GOD and then get rid of the besetting sin!

Fourth, **renounce** your sins let Satan know that you resign. Tell him I'm walking off the job and that you want no further connections with him! Sever your relationship with him at the head!

Fifth, cast him out! Good bye!

Sixth-renew you mind through the word of GOD!

> *Romans 12:2-Donot be conform to the pattern of this world, but be transformed by the renewing of your mind. **Then you** will be able to test and approve what GODS will is, his good pleasure and perfect will.*

Finally, it's time for a transformation! The renewing of your mind through GODS word will bring about this transformation! As we continue to dig in deep in prayer, praise, worship, studying GODS word and applying it to our lives we will be transformed into his image.

Maintain your deliverance! Stay delivered! Don't fall back into the same old habits, fulfilling the temptations of old things. I want you to know that just because GOD has delivered you does not mean that the tempter will not return to see if you are still holding fast to your confessions. Oh, he wants to know if you have any room left for him in your heart, in your mind and in your ways. He will be back!

> *Matthew 12:43-46 reads when an impure spirit comes out of a person, it goes through arid places seeking rest and does not find it.*

44. Then it says, "I will return to the house I left." When it arrives, it finds the house unoccupied, swept clean and put in order.

45. Then it goes and takes with it seven more spirits more wicked than itself and they go in and live there and the final state or condition of that person is worst that the first.

This part is so important because it tells us just who and what we are dealing with. It reveals to us the nature of the beast and that it will not stop because you cast it out once. Scripture tells us that it will return because it didn't want to let us go in the first place. If satan had his way none of us would be free, we would be enslaved by him for as long as he could have us. BUT GOD!

Friends I said all this to yet express how imperative it is to maintain what we have, what GOD through JESUS CHRIST has allowed us to enjoy and that is freedom in him! We need not think for a moment that the battle is over. We just have entered into another level and whenever we enter into another level we will certainly encounter more devils. In the end remember the WAR IS OURS! Let us rejoice in the victories of GOD while we prepare to enter in and win again!

I pray this has been the perfect appetizer and full course meal that you have been looking for my brothers and sisters! Thank you for dining with me today, I know I've enjoyed this meal myself! Maybe you are in a wonderful place with GOD but this book suites the fancy of someone you know. Someone who you have been praying and fasting with or even someone you've just been observing from afar. Whatever the case it is your responsibility to aid in whatever way you can a fellow brother or sister who is struggling and there are some things that are more precious than gold that we can impart into others. This book may be just the thing they need to exit out of the old and usher them into the new. Be a blessing and share the treasure you have found with someone else in need. Until next time may GOD richly bless you and those connected to you in JESUS NAME AMEN AND SO BE IT!

Printed in the United States
by Baker & Taylor Publisher Services